To

....

....

From

....

....

To Elliott and Austin with love

Library of Congress Control Number: 2023937933

ISBN 978-0-8091-6806-4 (hardcover)
ISBN 978-0-8091-8820-8 (e-book)

Published in North America under the title *A Child's Book of Blessings* by Paulist Press by arrangement with Lion Hudson IP Ltd
997 Macarthur Boulevard
Mahwah, New Jersey 07430

www.paulistpress.com

Printed and bound in China
by Dream Colour (Hong Kong) Printing Limited
Shenzhen, Guangdong
November 2023

A Child's Book of Blessings

Kenneth Steven
Illustrated by Katie Rewse

Paulist Press
New York / Mahwah, NJ

There is so much we want to give you,
but most of all we want to give you this blessing.
It comes with all the love in our hearts.

May you be blessed by the early morning
light that flows through the valley and wakens
the meadow and trees,

and brings the birds singing as the sun turns golden.

May you be blessed by the river as it journeys from the hills to the sea,

babbling its stories as it splashes your growing feet.

May you be blessed by the soft rain as it falls in a song
on the grass and the leaves and the roofs,

and you
listen to its
beautiful
notes in the
morning.

May you be blessed by the breeze as it grows wild in the winter and BOOMS about the house

and lifts your kite into the great winds of the sky.

May you be blessed by the sea as the waves
curl blue and green far out,

and then break, shining
on the sandy shore

where you run and dance.

May you be blessed by the rainbow that
arches over the fields in promise
after the rain has cleared,

showing that the sun will always come back, so you can go out to play once more.

May you be blessed by the snow that drifts like petals on the wind, and settles in every crack and crevice,

and makes the world white
for you to slide and skate and sled.

May you be blessed by the stars
that sparkle in the night skies
in their millions,
shining like silver breath
from north to south,
and east to west.

May you be blessed by God, who made all
these things for us to look after,

and to love and delight in all the days
of our lives.

Our words of blessing to you:

Let the heavens rejoice, let the earth be glad;
let the sea resound, and all that is in it.
Let the fields be jubilant, and everything in them;
let all the trees of the forest sing for joy.

Psalm 96:11-12

You will go out in joy
    and be led forth in peace;
the mountains and hills
    will burst into song before you,
and all the trees of the field
    will clap their hands.

Isaiah 55:12

The Lord bless you
        and keep you;
the Lord make his face shine on you
        and be gracious to you;
the Lord turn his face towards you
        and give you peace.

Numbers 6:24-26